FRENCH FRIES

FRENCH FRIES

ZAC WILLIAMS

GIBBS SMITH
TO ENRICH AND INSPIRE HUMANKIND

For Aimee
who always lets me have the last fry

First Edition
15 14 13 12 11   5 4 3 2 1

Text and photographs © 2011 Zac Williams

Saltado recipe on page 93 inspired by Nancy Page

Published by
Gibbs Smith
P.O. Box 667
Layton, Utah 84041

1.800.835.4993 orders
www.gibbs-smith.com
www.williamsvisual.com

Designed by Sheryl Dickert Smith
Printed and bound in Hong Kong
Gibbs Smith books are printed on paper produced from sustainable PEFC-certified forest/controlled wood source. Learn more at www.pefc.org.

Library of Congress Cataloging-in-Publication Data

Williams, Zac.
  French fries : recipes and photographs / by Zac Williams.
    p. cm.
  Includes index.
  ISBN 978-1-4236-0744-1
  1. French fries. 2. Dips (Appetizers) 3. Sauces. 4. Cookbooks. I. Title.
  TX803.P8W55 2011
  641.8'14—dc22
                    2010035250

Contents

Introduction

Simple foods serve as our daily companions throughout life. A slice of toast with jam for breakfast. Maybe the sandwich in our lunch box at school. Or a crisp salad with our dinner. These foods are like old friends that we take for granted but certainly miss when they're not around. They make everything else seem complete. In some sense, they give order to what we eat and, by extension, give us just a little more stability as we go about our lives.

Of all the foods we can count on, none is more universal than the french fry. A singular french fry is a stick of potato generally fried hot and crisp with a sprinkle of the oldest and simplest of seasonings: salt. When eaten in the plural, french fries are a small-change mini-feast served in a cardboard box that tempts us to indulge in finishing every last one. Maybe it is something ancestral that stirs inside us as we rejoice at the bounty of hot, salty deliciousness that sits before us. More is always better than less.

French fries are reliable. They can be counted on as a familiar taste regardless of whatever else might be on the menu. The french fry is usually a safe bet for the pickiest of palates, and it is the vegetable that children eat most. Millions of dollars are spent to ensure the consistency of your favorite fast-food fry.

Familiarity can lead to overlooking a truly unique potential. The fry often suffers this fate. Forever dunking it in ketchup, we miss the possibilities offered by this blank slate of sliced potato. When we use our imagination, the fry can be liberated to take on new flavors and structure. By combining the familiar with the exotic, we create food that is as delicious as it is fun.

The origins of the french fry are lost to history, although it is generally accepted that the fry as we know it came into being in Belgium or northern France sometime in the early nineteenth century. The evolution of the fry certainly began much earlier as Spanish conquistadors returned from the New World with the potato, which had been harvested for millennia in the regions around Peru. While viewed with much skepticism by the majority of Europeans for the next few hundred years, the potato finally gained acceptance in the late 1700s, assisted by celebrity supporters such as Marie Antoinette.

The french fry's popularity exploded in the United States following the First World War and the return of troops who had enjoyed the street food while in France and Belgium. When teamed with such popular convenience foods of the day as hot dogs and hamburgers, the french fry quickly became synonymous with a fast-paced lifestyle and good times. The advent of the automobile as the primary mode of transportation, particularly on the West Coast, began a new chapter in the life of the fry. Drive-ins and drive-thrus relied on the french fry as the sidecar to the burger.

The requirement for commercial fryers and equipment often stymied cooks attempting to prepare french fries at home, leaving the dish in the domain of professionals. With the better-equipped home kitchens of today, creating the simple french fry no longer stands as a challenge to all those who crave the taste of a perfect fry.

BASIC FRY RECIPES

POTATO BASICS

The best potato for french fries contains high solids and not a lot of water. The sugar content must be just right as well to produce a nice golden color. The flesh of the potato should be textured and full and never waxy. Fortunately, one of the most readily available potatoes, the Russet Burbank, fits these requirements perfectly.

The Russet Burbank is the most commonly cultivated potato in the United States today. The thin brown skin and earthy potato flavor are well suited to most dishes. Of most interest to prospective french fry cooks, the Russet Burbank has a high solid or starch content that cooks up fluffy and light.

Russet Burbank potatoes are generally sold in two grades: a number one and a number two. The number one grade is selected for uniform appearance and size and is packaged in a cardboard box. Potatoes are also graded for size determined by how many will fit in the fifty-pound carton. The ideal Russet Burbank for french fries is generally a 70-count potato, meaning a carton comes with 67 to 74 potatoes. This works out to be potatoes that are about 10 to 13 ounces each. The number two grade potato is packaged in burlap, paper, or plastic bags and doesn't have as good an appearance as a number one spud. Either grade will work magnificently for french fries.

Fresh unpeeled potatoes should be stored in a cool dark place at around 55 degrees F. Temperatures below 42 degrees F, such as those found in a refrigerator, cause the starch in potatoes to turn to sugar, which leads to discolored, lower-quality fries. Too much light can also cause greening of the potato due to the formation of chlorophyll. While harmless, the greening does detract from the beauty of a perfect fry and can taste bitter.

While the Russet Burbank is a great starting point, there is a wide world of potato varieties that can be used for french fries. The Bannock Russet is a recently cultivated potato that produces a generally lighter fry color due to a lower concentration of sugar. The Kennebec potato is the most popular for home gardeners and makes a delicious fresh-tasting fry.

Niche varieties such as the Ida Rose, Yukon Gold, and Yukon Rose are better suited to baking techniques, but all bring new colors and textures to the table when served as fries.

UNDERSTANDING OIL

Besides the star potato, the type of oil used for frying has the next biggest effect on the flavor and quality of a french fry. The ideal oil has a high smoke point and does not impart unpleasant flavors to the fry. In times past, beef tallow was considered the most delicious natural fat in which to cook fries. With the increased understanding of how different types of fats affect the health of our heart and circulatory systems, vegetable-based oils high in healthy unsaturated fats are now preferred.

The most common oil used in commercial kitchens is generally a vegetable oil derived from soy oil, which is high in polyunsaturated fats. It has a mild flavor and a high smoke point. Canola oil, pioneered in Canada, is produced from rapeseed and is also very commonly used. Canola oil can have a slightly more noticeable taste and odor when used to fry than peanut oil. However, it does offer the greatest potential health benefits with a high mono-unsaturated fat content including omega-3 acids. While canola oil is certainly very acceptable, I find I prefer a soy-based vegetable oil for deep-frying when a neutral flavor is needed.

My personal favorite oil for french fries is refined peanut oil. Peanut oil has a rich nutty taste that enhances the flavor of compatible foods such as fries and onion rings. It has a high smoke point and tends to have a more pleasant odor when heated. It also contains resveratrol, which is also found in the skin of red grapes and may be a beneficial anti-oxidant. Peanut oil adds a distinct flavor that can't be found in other oils.

Each cooking cycle in a deep-fryer lowers the smoke point of the oil used. For the best flavor and least odor, use fresh oil whenever possible. If oil is to be stored for reuse, all food particles should be filtered out of the cooled oil using cheesecloth or a fine mesh strainer. The used oil can be stored in a covered container in a cook dark place for up to two weeks.

By using proper cooking techniques, such as maintaining the correct cooking temperature, along with oils that are more heart healthy, home-cooked french fries can be a treat that we shouldn't feel guilty about indulging in.

EQUIPMENT AND TECHNIQUE

While any recipe in this book can be prepared in the basic home kitchen, there are a few pieces of kitchen equipment that can make fry preparation more enjoyable.

Deep-Fryer

The most important tool to invest in would be a good quality deep-fryer. A good deep-fryer is able to reheat the oil more quickly after a batch of fries are added, which gives more consistent results. A deep-fryer with a basket is preferred to allow a quick shake to drain away unwanted oil. The ability to accurately control temperature is also desirable, although you should verify as you cook with a suitable kitchen thermometer. For extended frying of any type, a quality deep-fryer will also have an integrated lid and odor filter. If possible, look for an oil capacity of one gallon and a heating element that is 1800 watts for the most consistency as you fry.

Deep-frying releases particles of oil into the air that can lead to unpleasant odors on furnishings and clothing. A good filter on a deep-fryer can reduce some of this odor. Cooking under a power-vented hood is the best option. If weather permits, an open window can also ventilate the kitchen. In the summer months, outdoor frying is particularly enjoyable, either using a propane stove or burner or even a side grill burner that has sufficient heat output.

Be careful while deep frying to avoid burns and fire. Never add frozen food directly to a deep-fryer as it may result in a boil over. Make certain that the deep-fryer is on a stable, heat-resistant surface such as a range top. In the event of a fire, never use water to quench the flames. Keep a kitchen fire-extinguisher readily available. Be mindful of any children and take precaution to keep them safely away from hot oil.

Thermometer

A quick-read quality kitchen thermometer suitable for high-temperature deep-frying is critical in being able to consistently reproduce good fry results in the home kitchen.

Fry Cutter

For extended fry making, a professional fry cutter is a great option. Available at restaurant supply stores, fry cutters make quick work of turning potatoes into sticks. They are available with interchanging cutters to determine fry thickness, usually in the range of 1/4 to 1/2 inch. A sharp cutter or knife is critical in preventing microscopic jagged edges on the potato, which can result in the fries breaking while cooking.

Shakers

An assortment of shaker containers is helpful for various seasoning mixes. With the right selection of seasonings, one batch of fries can taste four or five different ways.

FROZEN FRIES

A fresh french fry has that special superior flavor, but oftentimes other restraints can limit our time in the kitchen. One solution is to make a double batch of The Essential French Fry (page 16) and freeze in heavy-weight ziplock bags after the first blanching in oil. The frozen fries can be placed in the refrigerator the night before you want to cook them and then deep-fried fresh when needed.

If this isn't practical, it is best to find a food-service-quality frozen french fry that is minimally processed and follow the instructions for preparation. The prepared fries can then be used in any of the recipes in this book.

SERVING SUGGESTIONS

There really isn't such a thing as a good cold french fry. It is critical to maintain the hot temperature that makes a homemade fry in particular so remarkable. The best way to do this is to have hungry guests standing by as the fries come out. Alternately preheat the oven to 225 degrees F and hold the fries on a baking sheet for a few minutes until ready. This is particularly useful when making many of the recipes in this book that require more preparation.

One of the best things about french fries is the fun that we have eating them! Be creative in serving fries in ways that enhance their appeal. An easy method is to make paper cones out of baking parchment and tape. Fill the cones with hot fries and hand them to guests to enjoy. You can also secure a supply of paper dishes and condiment cups from local diners and drive-ins by asking for a few extras. Paper cups and small brown paper bags are also great ways to serve a lot of people delicious fries without a lot of cleanup. When entertaining, try a fry bar for a unique twist. Make several different types of dipping sauces, seasonings, and fry toppings available for guests to try.

There is no wrong way to eat a french fry, so have fun and experiment. Enjoy!

Basic Fry Recipes

THE ESSENTIAL FRENCH FRY

This is the starting point—the basic french fry that is crisp on the outside and fluffy in the middle. This is the fry perfected in street stands for over two centuries in Belgium and France. Master this fry and you'll have no problem finding friends.

6 fresh No. 1 Idaho Russet Burbank potatoes (12 to 15 ounces each)

2 teaspoons white vinegar

Peanut oil

Sea salt

CUT AND RINSE

Peel the potatoes and cut them into lengths a little less than $1/2$ inch square using a knife with a sharp blade or a fry cutter. Place the cut potatoes in a large bowl filled with cold water. Add the vinegar and swirl the potatoes around. Place the bowl in the refrigerator for at least 1 hour. Swirl the potatoes again and drain the water. Spread the potatoes on a layer of paper towels and pat dry with additional paper towels.

FIRST FRY

In a large heavy pot or deep-fryer, preheat the peanut oil to 315 degrees F. Use a kitchen thermometer to verify the temperature. In small batches, approximately 2 cups each, add the sliced potatoes to the hot oil. Cook for 5 to 7 minutes until just tender but not brown. Using a basket, remove the potato slices from the oil, shaking to remove excess oil. Spread the potatoes on a sheet pan lined with paper towels to drain. At this point the potato slices should be refrigerated at least 1 hour, uncovered, or as long as overnight. You can also freeze the blanched slices at this stage for up to 1 month in a well-sealed freezer bag.

SECOND FRY

When you are ready to serve the fries, reheat the oil to 375 degrees F and fry the potato slices for about 4 minutes until crispy and golden. (If using frozen potatoes, allow them to thaw before frying.) Remove from the fryer, shaking the basket to remove excess oil. Spread on paper towels. Allow the fries to stand for 1 minute before salting. Serve with any of the accompaniments in the Dips and Sauces chapter as desired. Serves 6

THE DRIVE-IN FRY

The automobile revolutionized just about everything, including the way we eat. The drive-in and its closely related cousin the drive-thru took America's love of the car and combined it with french fries, which are perfect for eating at the wheel. Who hasn't reached into the bottom of the bag while driving to pull out fingerfuls of hot fries to eat?

8 fresh Kennebec potatoes (Russet Burbank may be substituted)

Vegetable oil

Sea salt

Fry Sauce (page 104)

CUT AND RINSE

Peel the potatoes and cut them into lengths about $1/4$ inch square using a knife with a sharp blade or a fry cutter. Place the cut potatoes in a large bowl filled with cold water. Swirl the potatoes around. Drain and repeat. Spread the potatoes on a layer of paper towels and pat dry with additional paper towels.

FRY

In a large heavy pot or deep-fryer, preheat the vegetable oil to 365 degrees F. Use a kitchen thermometer to verify the temperature. In small batches, approximately 2 cups each, add the sliced potatoes to the hot oil. Cook for about 5 minutes until crisp and slightly brown. Using a basket, remove the potato slices from the oil, shaking to remove excess oil. Spread the potatoes on a sheet pan lined with paper towels to drain. Allow the fries to stand for 1 minute before salting. Serve with Fry Sauce. Serves 6

THE OVEN FRY

Oven fries often are seen as the compromise fry: better for you, but not as tasty. This doesn't have to be the case. Properly prepared oven fries can stand tall in the pantheon of classic french fries.

6 fresh thin-skinned red potatoes

¼ cup extra virgin olive oil

2 teaspoons fresh parsley

1 tablespoon paprika

Sea salt

Black pepper to taste

Homemade Ketchup (page 107)

Cover a baking sheet with aluminum foil, spray with nonstick cook spray and place in the oven. Preheat oven to 425 degrees F.

CUT

Scrub and wash the potatoes. Cut them lengthwise into wedges, halving and then quartering to create 8 fries from each potato.

MIX

In a mixing bowl combine the olive oil, parsley, and paprika. Add the potato wedges and toss to coat. Carefully remove the hot baking sheet from the oven and dump the potatoes from the bowl onto the sheet, spreading in a single layer.

BAKE

Return baking sheet to oven and bake potatoes for 30 to 35 minutes, stirring the potatoes and shaking the pan occasionally. Cook until the potatoes are brown on the outside and soft on the inside. Serve with Homemade Ketchup. Serves 6

THE SWEET FRY

The sweet potato or yam (the oranger, softer variety) is rich in vitamins and taste. I like to think of the sweet potato as a dessert that is part of the meal.

4 large sweet potatoes or yams

1/2 cup Vanilla Sugar*

2 teaspoons cinnamon

Vegetable oil

Caramel Sauce (page 108)

Make Vanilla Sugar by storing several cups of sugar in a closed container for at least a week with a vanilla bean that has been split open. Vanilla Sugar is great for use in all types of desserts.

CUT

Peel the sweet potatoes and cut them into lengths about 1/4 inch square using a knife with a sharp blade.

MIX

Mix the Vanilla Sugar and cinnamon together in a small bowl.

FRY

In a large heavy pot or deep-fryer, preheat the vegetable oil to 365 degrees F. Use a kitchen thermometer to verify the temperature. In small batches, approximately 2 cups each, add the sliced sweet potatoes to the hot oil. Cook for about 5 minutes until crisp and brown. Using a basket, remove the sweet potato fries from the oil, shaking to remove excess oil. Spread the fries on a sheet pan lined with paper towels to drain. Allow the fries to stand for 1 minute and sprinkle with the sugar and cinnamon mixture. Repeat for the remaining batches. Serve with Caramel Sauce. Serves 6

THE HOMESTYLE FRY

If I could have just one type of fry, this would be it. Skin-on potato fries have an earthy taste that goes well with just about any comfort food. The slight tang of buttermilk and the battered crunch of these fries should not be missed.

6 fresh Idaho Russet Burbank
   potatoes (12 to 15 ounces each)

2 cups all-purpose flour

2 teaspoons baking powder

2 cups buttermilk

2 teaspoons garlic salt

1 teaspoon chopped fresh parsley

Peanut oil

Sea salt

Barbecue Mayonnaise (page 111)

CUT AND RINSE

Scrub and wash the potatoes. Leaving the skin on, cut the potatoes into lengths a little less than $1/2$ inch square using a knife with a sharp blade or a fry cutter. Place the cut potatoes in a large bowl filled with cold water. Swirl the potatoes around. Drain and repeat. Spread the potatoes on a layer of paper towels and pat dry with additional paper towels.

MIX

Combine the flour, garlic salt, and baking powder in a large ziplock bag. Pour the buttermilk in a bowl.

FRY

In a large heavy pot or deep-fryer, preheat the peanut oil to 365 degrees F. Use a kitchen thermometer to verify the temperature. In small batches, approximately 2 cups each, dunk the potato slices in the buttermilk and then add to the ziplock bag. Carefully seal the bag and then

Recipe continued on following page.

shake with the flour mixture until coated. Add the coated
potato slices to the hot oil. Cook for 5 to 7 minutes until
crisp. Using a basket, remove from the fryer, shaking
the basket to remove excess oil. Spread on paper towels.
Allow the fries to stand for 1 minute before salting.
Sprinkle with chopped fresh parsley. Serve with Barbecue
Mayonnaise. Serves 6

French Fry Favorites

CAJUN-STYLE FRIES

Once you've mastered the art of the simple fry, you can take it up a notch simply by substituting different spice mixes for salt. These Cajun-Style Fries are a good place to start.

1 recipe Essential Fries (page 16),
  Oven Fries (page 20), or
  Homestyle Fries (page 25)

1/4 cup salt

2 tablespoons paprika

2 tablespoons onion powder

1 tablespoon cayenne pepper

1 tablespoon white pepper

1 tablespoon garlic powder

1 teaspoon thyme

Dash ground cloves

Combine all spices and store in a covered container. Place in a shaker to sprinkle on prepared fries in place of salt. Serve Cajun-Style Fries with ketchup.

BEACH FRIES

Served on the boardwalks of Atlantic beaches, these simple fries are a taste of summer.

1 recipe Essential Fries (page 16)
   or Drive-in Fries (page 18)

Old Bay Seasoning

Apple cider vinegar

Make fries according to directions. When fries are finished cooking, sprinkle with Old Bay Seasoning instead of salt. Serve in a paper cup, dousing liberally with apple cider vinegar.

PHILLY CHEESE FRIES

Derived from the famous cheese steak sandwich, this recipe is a quick way to add flavor to fries for a game night party.

1 recipe Essential Fries (page 16)
or Drive-in Fries (page 18)

1 teaspoon butter or margarine

1 small onion, minced

1 bottle Cheez Whiz

In a small sauté pan over medium heat, cook the butter and onion until brown. Heat the Cheez Whiz in the microwave following instructions on the label. In individual paper trays or bowls, place servings of prepared french fries and top with Cheez Whiz followed by the sautéed onion.

PARMESAN FRIES

Parmesan cheese and fresh parsley combine for a simple, yet delicious fry that's a great accompaniment to a juicy grilled burger or steak.

1 recipe Essential Fries (page 16)

1 cup finely grated Parmigiano-Reggiano or other Parmesan cheese

2 tablespoons chopped fresh Italian parsley

Make fries according to directions. When fries are finished cooking, toss with the Parmesan cheese and parsley instead of salt. This recipe is particularly good with a thicker cut fry.

GARLIC FRIES

A longtime staple of ballparks and stadiums, garlic fries are simple to make and delicious to eat. Substitute $1/2$ teaspoon of prepared diced garlic in place of each clove for an easy-to-store alternative to fresh garlic.

1 recipe Essential Fries (page 16),
   Drive-in Fries (page 18),
   Oven Fries (page 20), or
   Homestyle Fries (page 25)

2 cloves garlic, minced

2 teaspoons olive oil

1 teaspoon chopped
   fresh rosemary

2 teaspoons chopped fresh parsley

Sauté the garlic in the olive oil in a small pan over medium heat until the garlic is translucent. Remove from heat and add rosemary and parsley.

Make fries according to directions. When fries are finished cooking, instead of salt toss with garlic mixture in a large bowl.

BUFFALO FRIES

These spicy and tangy fries have a puffy, crispy shell that is complemented by the blue cheese dip that also tastes great with traditional hot wings.

6 fresh Russet potatoes

Peanut oil

1 cup flour

$^1/_2$ cup buttermilk

2 teaspoons Louisiana-style hot sauce

1 teaspoon salt

$^1/_2$ teaspoon black pepper

$^1/_2$ teaspoon garlic powder

$^1/_2$ teaspoon paprika

Sea salt

Blue Cheese Dip (page 111)

Peel and cut the potatoes into 3 inch lengths about $^1/_2$ inch square using a knife with a sharp blade.

In a deep-fryer, or heavy pot, preheat the peanut oil to 325 degrees F. Add the cut potatoes and cook about 5 minutes until soft but not browned. Remove and drain the excess oil; spread the slices on a sheet pan lined with paper towels. Set aside.

Combine the flour, buttermilk, hot sauce, salt, pepper, and spices in a bowl and mix well.

Increase the temperature of the peanut oil to 375 degrees F. Use a kitchen thermometer to verify the temperature. In small batches, approximately 2 cups each, coat the potato pieces with the batter.

Add the battered potatoes to the hot oil using cooking tongs, being careful not to overcrowd the fries. Cook for about 5 minutes until crisp and slightly brown. Using a

Recipe continued on following page.

basket remove the potatoes slices from the oil, shaking to remove any excess. Spread the potatoes on a sheet pan lined with paper towels to drain. Allow the fries to stand for 1 minute before salting with sea salt. Serve with Blue Cheese Dip.

OVEN SWEET POTATO CHIPS

Healthy and delicious, sweet potatoes are full flavored enough that a simple toss in olive oil with a little dash of cumin is all that is needed to make a delicious chip.

2 large sweet potatoes or yams

2 tablespoons olive oil

1 teaspoon cumin

1 teaspoon sea salt

Teriyaki Mayonnaise (page 121)

Cover a baking sheet with aluminum foil and place in the oven. Preheat oven to 450 degrees F.

Peel the sweet potatoes and cut them into thin, round slices about $\frac{1}{8}$ inch thick.

In a large bowl, combine the olive oil, cumin, and salt. Add the sweet potato slices and toss to coat.

Dump the slices onto the baking sheet and bake for 10 minutes until the edges begin to blacken. Serve with Teriyaki Mayonnaise.

TEXAS CHEDDAR FRIES

My first introduction to true cheddar fries happened in Dallas at a local lunch spot famous for bowls of fries piled high with cheese, bacon, and jalapeños served with a healthy side of homemade ranch dressing.

1 recipe Essential Fries (page 16)
  or Homestyle Fries (page 25)

2 cups shredded sharp
  cheddar cheese

1 cup cooked and crumbled bacon

1 small can jalapeño pepper
  slices, drained

Ranch Dressing (page 112)

Divide prepared fries among six individual ovenproof bowls. Top each with $\frac{1}{3}$ cup shredded cheese, a little crumbled bacon, and a few jalapeño slices. Place in a broiler on high for 2 to 3 minutes to melt the cheese. Serve with Ranch Dressing on the side for dipping.

FRESH GREEN BEAN FRIES

This twist on the french fry combines a savory taste of summer with a pleasant crunch.

2 pounds fresh green beans,
    washed and snapped

2 eggs

2 cups panko bread crumbs

2 teaspoons sea salt

2 teaspoons white pepper

Peanut oil

Horseradish Sauce (page 117)

Mix the eggs in a shallow dish. Combine the panko crumbs with the salt and white pepper in another dish.

In a large heavy pot or deep-fryer, preheat the oil to 365 degrees F. Use a kitchen thermometer to verify the temperature.

In small batches, approximately 2 cups each, dredge the green beans in the egg mixture and then roll in the bread crumb mixture.

Using kitchen tongs, add the green beans to the hot oil in small batches. Cook for about 5 minutes until crisp and slightly brown. Using a basket, remove the green beans from the oil, shaking to remove any excess. Spread the green beans on a sheet pan lined with paper towels to drain. Serve with Horseradish Sauce.

BALSAMIC POMMES FRITES AND PORK CHOP

French fries need not be only a fast-food fare. The sweet and rich flavor of the balsamic reduction soaks into the potato for an elegant, easy-to-make dinner.

2 fresh No. 1 Idaho Russet Burbank
   potatoes (12 to 15 ounces each)

4 tablespoons olive oil

2 tablespoons kosher salt

4 boneless pork chops

1 cup balsamic vinegar

2 teaspoons chopped
   fresh rosemary

Peel and slice the potatoes in rectangular strips $3/4$ inch wide by $1/4$ inch high. Add the oil to a large skillet over medium-high heat and bring to about 350 degrees F. Add the potato strips in a single layer and fry until soft, about 8 minutes. Remove potatoes and keep warm in a 250 degrees F oven.

Rub salt into both sides of the pork chops and add to skillet. Reduce heat and cook over medium for about 6 minutes per side or until 155 degrees F is reached internally at the thickest part of the chop as shown by a meat thermometer.

Turn heat to low and add the balsamic vinegar. Reduce for about 2 minutes until thickened. Remove the pork chops and add the cooked potatoes, stirring to coat with the balsamic reduction. Garnish with the chopped fresh rosemary and serve immediately.

SWEET ONION FRIES

Mild, yet full of flavor, these sweet onion fries are a quick and easy way to create an unexpected combination. This is a great side dish to classic Southern chicken and waffles.

1 recipe Essential Fries (page 16),
   Oven Fries (page 20), or
   Homestyle Fries (page 25)

1 large sweet onion, finely chopped

1 tablespoon butter

$1/2$ cup American Parmesan
   grated cheese

Sweet Onion Mayonnaise
   (page 121)

Sauté the onion in a skillet with the butter for 3 minutes over medium-high heat until just beginning to soften.

Add the prepared french fries in batches to a large mixing bowl and toss with the onion mixture and the Parmesan cheese. Serve with Sweet Onion Mayonnaise.

PUB ONION RINGS

Onion rings always seem to be the upgrade to french fries. The hearty beer batter on these rings makes them a great appetizer for a casual meal.

12 ounces amber ale

2 cups flour

1 egg yolk, beaten

$1/2$ teaspoon white pepper

$3/4$ teaspoon salt

4 large sweet onions

Peanut oil

Ranch Dressing (page 112)

Whisk together all of the ingredients in a large bowl except the onions.

Slice the onions into rings about $3/4$ inch thick. Separate into rings and dip into the batter. Using tongs, place small batches of onion rings in the deep-fryer and cook at 365 degrees F for about 4 minutes or until golden brown. Serve with Ranch Dressing.

GREEN CHILE FRIES

The full flavor of green chiles is balanced by the fresh, salty queso blanco. You can find canned tomatillos at a Latin food market or in the ethnic section of some supermarkets.

1 recipe Essential Fries (page 16),
　　Oven Fries (page 20), or
　　Homestyle Fries (page 25)

1 small can green chiles, undrained

1 small can tomatillos,
　　drained and chopped

1 clove garlic, chopped

$1/2$ teaspoon black pepper

$1/2$ teaspoon cumin

1 cup crumbled queso
　　blanco or queso fresco

Fresh cilantro (optional)

In a small saucepan over medium heat, combine the green chiles, tomatillos, garlic, pepper, and cumin. Sauté for 5 minutes until heated and fragrant. Transfer to a food processor or blender and blend until smooth. Reheat in saucepan if necessary.

Pour chile sauce over servings of prepared fries and top with the crumbled queso. Garnish with cilantro if desired.

CINCINNATI CHILI CHEESE FRIES

Cincinnati chili is a unique regional meat stew that doesn't rely on traditional chili powder for flavor. Served most famously over spaghetti, it is also delicious over fries.

1 recipe Essential Fries (page 16)
   or Oven Fries (page 20)

1 (15-ounce) can Cincinnati chili
   (no beans) or other beanless chili

2 cups shredded sharp
   cheddar cheese

1 small onion, finely minced

Heat the chili in a saucepan over medium heat. Make fries according to directions. Divide among serving plates. Pour chili over hot french fries and top with cheese and minced onion.

NACHO FRIES

A meal in itself, Nacho Fries are a heartier alternative to the tortilla chip variety.

1 recipe Essential Fries (page 16),
    Oven Fries (page 20), or
    Homestyle Fries (page 25)

1 cup shredded sharp
    cheddar cheese

1 cup shredded Monterey
    Jack cheese

2 cups cooked shredded
    beef, warmed

2 roma tomatoes,
    seeded and diced

1 can black olives,
    drained and sliced

1 cup sour cream

1 cup guacamole

Bottled salsa

Make fries according to directions and place on an ovenproof serving platter. Top with shredded cheeses and beef. Broil on high, six inches from the broiler, for about 3 minutes or until cheese is melted. Top with tomatoes, olives, sour cream, and guacamole. Serve with salsa for dipping.

OVEN ASPARAGUS FRIES

While probably not considered a true fry, this very easy recipe is delicious, healthy, and perfect paired with an easy-to-make lemon butter sauce.

2 pounds tender young
  asparagus, washed and trimmed

2 teaspoons olive oil

Sea salt

Fresh black pepper

Lemon Butter Sauce (page 125)

Preheat oven to 450 degrees F. Cover a baking sheet with parchment or aluminum foil.

Toss the asparagus with the olive oil. Spread on the baking sheet and sprinkle with salt and pepper. Bake for 10 minutes and serve immediately. Pair with Lemon Butter Sauce.

PESTO FRIES

Pesto has an intense flavor that perfectly complements the starchy french fry. For an easy shortcut, use a quality prepared pesto from the grocery store.

1 recipe Essential Fries (page 16), Drive-in Fries (page 18), or Oven Fries (page 20)

1 cup fresh basil leaves, packed

$^1/_2$ cup pine nuts

2 cloves garlic, minced

$^1/_2$ teaspoon salt

$^1/_2$ cup extra virgin olive oil

1 cup freshly grated Parmesan or other hard cheese

Combine basil, pine nuts, garlic, and salt in a food processor. Process until a paste forms. While pulsing the food processor, slowly pour in olive oil until combined with paste.

Make fries according to directions. Mix pesto with hot fries and toss to coat. Sprinkle with grated cheese before serving.

CHOCOLATE FRIES

French fries and chocolate are one of those strange combinations that defy expectations and taste delicious together for a decadent treat. This rich and nuanced chocolate sauce is also great on ice cream.

1 recipe Essential Fries (page 16), Drive-in Fries (page 18), or Oven Fries (page 20)

1/2 stick unsalted butter

1/4 cup semisweet chocolate pieces

1 cup sugar

1/4 cup high quality cocoa

1/2 cup heavy cream

1/4 teaspoon salt

1/2 tablespoon vanilla extract

In a saucepan over medium heat, melt the butter and add the chocolate pieces, stirring frequently to melt. Once melted, whisk in the sugar and cocoa, followed by the cream. Continue to stir, bring to a boil, and remove from heat. Stir in the salt and vanilla. Serve warm as a dipping sauce for the prepared french fries.

FONTINA AND SUN-DRIED TOMATO FRIES

Fontina's salty, nutty taste is something that I often crave.

1 recipe Essential Fries (page 16)
   or Oven Fries (page 20)

¼ cup whole milk

¼ cup white wine

¼ cup finely chopped
   sun-dried tomatoes

1 cup grated fontina cheese

In a heavy bottomed saucepan over medium heat, combine the milk, white wine, and sun-dried tomatoes. Bring the mixture just to a boil. While constantly stirring, add small handfuls of the grated cheese, stirring constantly until it melts. Pour over prepared french fries to serve.

POTATO CORKSCREWS

Thin and tasty, Potato Corkscrews are fun to make, especially for children.

2 fresh No. 1 Idaho Russet Burbank
    potatoes (12 to 15 ounces each)

2 teaspoons white vinegar

Peanut oil

Sea salt

Peel the potatoes. Using a good clean potato peeler, cut long curly strips lengthwise from the potato. Alternately, an apple peeler also works great for this.

Place the potato strips in a large bowl filled with cold water. Add the vinegar and swirl the potatoes around to remove excess starch. Drain the water. Spread the potatoes on a layer of paper towels and pat dry with additional paper towels.

In a large heavy pot or deep-fryer, preheat the oil to 365 degrees F. Use a kitchen thermometer to verify the temperature. In small batches, approximately 2 cups each, add the potato curls to the hot oil. Cook for about 3 minutes until crisp and brown. Using a basket, remove the potato corkscrews from the oil, shaking to remove any excess. Spread the potato curls on a sheet pan lined with paper towels to drain.

Allow the fries to stand for 1 minute and then salt. Serve immediately or store in a covered container for up to three days.

TOFU FRIES

Who would have thought that tofu could make a delicious fry that is high in protein and tastes great? The secret is the crispy shell that the cornstarch creates.

1 pound extra firm tofu

¹/₂ cup tamari soy sauce

¹/₂ cup cornstarch

Peanut oil

Raspberry Ginger Dipping
    Sauce (page 125)

Slice the tofu into fry-shaped strips. Put the soy sauce in a shallow bowl and the cornstarch in a second shallow bowl. Dip the tofu fries in the soy sauce and then roll them in the cornstarch to cover all sides.

In a large heavy pot or deep-fryer, preheat the oil to 355 degrees F. Using tongs, place the tofu in the oil and deep-fry for about 4 minutes until crispy and brown. Using a basket, remove the fries from the oil, shaking to remove any excess. Spread the fries on a baking sheet lined with paper towels to drain. Serve with Raspberry Ginger Dipping Sauce.

MUSTARD FRIES

The fry with a sweet-and-sour kick!

1 recipe Essential Fries (page 16), Oven Fries (page 20), or Homestyle Fries (page 25)

1 teaspoon powdered mustard

1 tablespoon sugar

1 teaspoon kosher salt

1 tablespoon dried parsley

Combine all dry ingredients in a bowl. Make fries according to directions. Instead of salting, toss hot fries with mustard salt to coat.

MIDWEST POTATO CHIPS

Potato chips have become somewhat overly perfected. This more rustic version takes the potato chip a little closer to its common ancestor, the fry.

6 fresh No. 1 Idaho Russet Burbank potatoes (12 to 15 ounces each)

Peanut oil

Sea salt

2 teaspoons oregano

Scrub and wash the potatoes, but do not peel. Slice into thin rounds. Place the cut potatoes in a large bowl filled with ice water. Swirl the potatoes around. Drain and repeat. Spread the potatoes on a layer of paper towels and pat dry with additional paper towels.

In a large heavy pot or deep-fryer, preheat the peanut oil to 375 degrees F. Use a kitchen thermometer to verify the temperature. In small batches, approximately 2 cups each, add the sliced potatoes to the hot oil. Cook for about 5 minutes until crisp and brown. Using a basket, remove the potato slices from the oil, shaking to remove any excess. Spread the potatoes on a sheet pan lined with paper towels to drain. Allow the chips to stand for 1 minute before salting. Sprinkle with salt and oregano. May be covered and stored up to two days.

BREAKFAST FRIES

This is a great way to use up leftover oven fries. Reheat in the same skillet used for the bacon and eggs.

1 recipe Essential Fries (page 16),
    Homestyle Fries (page 25),
    or Oven Fries (page 20)

4 eggs

8 strips cooked bacon

1 cup shredded Swiss cheese

1 cup fresh salsa

In a skillet over medium-high heat, cook the eggs over easy, leaving the yolk soft. On four serving plates place a portion of prepared fries, two strips of bacon, a cooked egg, and $\frac{1}{4}$ cup shredded cheese. Serve with a $\frac{1}{4}$ cup fresh salsa on the side.

International Flavors

SLAP CHIPS

This is the South African take on the french fry. *Slap* means "soft" in Afrikaans. These chips should be crispy on the outside, soft on the inside, and drenched in vinegar.

8 fresh Russet potatoes
(8 to 12 ounces each)

2 cups white vinegar

Peanut oil

Sea salt

Malt vinegar

Peel and cut the potatoes into lengths a little less than $1/2$ inch square using a knife with a sharp blade. Place the cut potatoes into a bowl with the white vinegar. Allow to sit for 10 minutes, stirring occasionally. Drain the vinegar and spread the potatoes on a layer of paper towels; pat dry with additional paper towels.

In a large heavy pot or in a deep-fryer, preheat the peanut oil to 350 degrees F. Use a kitchen thermometer to verify the temperature. In small batches, approximately 2 cups each, add the cut potatoes to the hot oil. Cook for 5 to 7 minutes until just tender but not brown. Using a basket, remove the potatoes from the oil, shaking to remove any excess. Spread the potatoes on a sheet pan lined with paper towels to drain.

Reheat the oil to 375 degrees F and fry the potatoes a second time for about 4 minutes until crispy and golden. Remove from the fryer, shaking the basket to remove excess oil. Spread on paper towels. Allow the fries to stand for 1 minute before salting. Serve in paper bags or wrapping sprinkled liberally with malt vinegar.

POUTINE

A national Canadian fry dish that originated in Quebec, poutine is a meal in itself of thick-cut fries, gravy, and fresh cheese curd. It is often served in school cafeterias as well as in all types of eating establishments. In the eastern United States, a similar dish is known as disco fries.

1 recipe Essential Fries (page 16)

2 cups prepared turkey gravy

2 cups fresh cheese curd

Place prepared french fries on 6 individual serving plates and sprinkle each with ⅓ cup cheese curds. Pour ⅓ cup hot gravy over the fries and curds, and serve immediately.

GREEK FRIES

Pairing feta cheese with the tang of red wine vinegar is a classic Greek flavor that clings perfectly to potato fries.

1 recipe Essential Fries (page 16) or Oven Fries (page 20)

$^1/_2$ cup red wine vinegar

1 teaspoon finely minced garlic

2 teaspoons chopped fresh basil

2 teaspoons chopped fresh oregano

1 teaspoon onion powder

1 cup crumbled feta cheese, plus more for garnish

Tzatziki Sauce (page 115)

Combine the red wine vinegar, garlic, herbs, and onion powder in a bowl.

When fries are finished cooking, place in batches in a large ziplock bag with 2 tablespoons of the red wine vinegar mixture and 2 tablespoons feta cheese. Toss to coat. Place on plates and sprinkle with more feta cheese. Serve with Tzatziki Sauce.

FRENCH FRY WAR (PATATJE OORLOG)

While the Belgians are the per capita fry-consuming champs of Europe, the Dutch are not far behind. French Fry War is a snack bar standby that features fries served with a variety—and occasionally all—of the condiments offered. The fun part is deciding which sauce is the victor. In any case, it is usually your taste buds that win!

1 recipe Essential Fries (page 16)

Satay Sauce (page 116)

Curry Ketchup (page 117)

Speciaal Sauce (page 116)

As soon as the fries come out of the fryer and are drained, place one serving on a deep plate. Quickly place three equal large spoonfuls each of Satay Sauce, Curry Ketchup, and Speciaal Sauce on the fries. Serve immediately.

TEMPURA VEGETABLES

Tempura may be the distant relative of the french fry. The Japanese have long enjoyed the crispy, crunchy taste of fresh vegetables coated with a fluffy batter.

3/4 cup flour

1/4 cup cornstarch

2 tablespoons baking powder

1 teaspoon sea salt

1 egg yolk

3/4 cup club soda, chilled

Peanut oil

Carrots and potatoes, sliced into 3/8 inch sticks

Onion, sliced and separated into rings

Mushrooms

Broccoli florets

Toasted sesame seeds

Wasabi Garlic Mayonnaise (page 118)

In a large bowl, mix all ingredients except the vegetables and sesame seeds, adding egg yolk and club soda last. Whisk to form a smooth batter.

Preheat the oil to 375 degrees F in a heavy pot or deep-fryer. Dip the vegetables in the batter, shaking off excess. Then fry in small batches for about 2 to 3 minutes until puffy, golden, and cooked through. Drain on paper towels.

Sprinkle with toasted sesame seeds. Serve tempura with Wasabi Garlic Mayonnaise for dipping.

NEWFIE FRIES

Another Canadian fry favorite, this time from Newfoundland. Newfie fries are a Thanksgiving dinner on the go.

1 recipe Essential Fries (page 16), Drive-in Fries (page 18), or Homestyle Fries (page 25)

1 box prepared sage stuffing mix

2 cups cooked green peas

3 cups turkey gravy

On 6 individual serving plates, divide the prepared french fries. Cover with $\frac{1}{2}$ cup stuffing and $\frac{1}{3}$ cup peas. Pour $\frac{1}{2}$ cup hot gravy over the fries, stuffing, and peas, and serve immediately.

BISTEC A LO POBRE

A popular dish originating in Chile that loosely translates as "Poor Man's Steak."

1 recipe Essential Fries (page 16),
  Oven Fries (page 20), or
  Homestyle Fries (page 25)

2 cloves garlic, minced

2 tablespoons paprika

2 tablespoons oregano

1 teaspoon cumin

1 tablespoon salt

4 (8-ounce) sirloin steaks,
  about $^{1}/_{2}$ inch thick each

2 onions, sliced into rings

1 teaspoon olive oil

4 eggs

Combine the garlic, paprika, oregano, cumin, and salt in a bowl. Rub the steaks well on both sides with the mixture.

On a medium grill, cook the steaks for about 6 minutes on each side, checking with a meat thermometer for doneness. Medium-well should register about 155 degrees F.

While cooking the steaks, sauté the onion in a nonstick pan over medium-high heat in the olive oil for about 5 minutes until soft and translucent. Transfer the onions to a bowl and keep warm.

Add the eggs one at a time to the pan and fry sunny side up, leaving the yolks soft.

When ready to serve, layer the prepared fries on serving plates and top with cooked onion, a steak, and finally a fried egg. Serve with Chilean Salad (page 89) on the side.

CHILEAN SALAD

A fresh side dish that complements Bistec a lo Pobre.

3 cups roughly chopped
   ripe tomatoes

1 cup finely sliced red
   or sweet onion

2 teaspoons lime juice

2 tablespoons extra virgin olive oil

2 tablespoons chopped fresh
   cilantro, plus more for garnish

Salt

Freshly ground black pepper

Combine all ingredients in a bowl and season to taste with the salt and black pepper. Garnish with more cilantro. Serves 4

MASALA FRIES

Masala is a blend of spices used in cooking in Indian, Pakistani, and other South Asian cultures. Fragrant and multifaceted masala is perfect for an exotic fry dish.

1 recipe Essential Fries (page 16), Drive-in Fries (page 18), or Oven Fries (page 20)

2 tablespoons olive oil

2 onions, finely chopped

2 cloves garlic, minced

1 green bell pepper, finely chopped

2 tomatoes, seeded and diced

1 can chickpeas, undrained

1 teaspoon coriander

2 teaspoons cumin

1 teaspoon turmeric

1/2 teaspoon ground cloves

2 teaspoons ground ginger

Fresh cilantro

In a skillet over medium heat, add the olive oil, onion, garlic, and green pepper. Sauté for about 5 minutes until the onion is soft.

Add the tomatoes, chickpeas, and the seasonings reserving the fresh ginger. Simmer for another 10 minutes until the sauce thickens and the flavors blend. In the last minute of cooking, add the ginger. Serve over individual servings of prepared french fries. Garnish with fresh cilantro.

SALTADO

Saltado is an extremely popular main course meal in Peru. It is made with beef or chicken and usually with a side of white rice.

1 recipe Essential Fries (page 16), Drive-in Fries (page 18), or Oven Fries (page 20)

1 cup white vinegar

2 teaspoons salt

1 teaspoon freshly ground black pepper

3 garlic cloves, pressed

4 chicken breasts

2 tablespoons olive oil

2 ripe tomatoes, sliced

1 yellow onion, sliced

1 aji or Peruvian hot pepper, cut into thin strips (a jalapeño or yellow pepper may be substituted)

Prepared white rice

Fresh cilantro

Combine the vinegar, salt, pepper, and garlic to create a marinade. Cut the chicken into thin strips and place in the marinade. Refrigerate for 24 hours for the best flavor.

Heat the olive oil in a skillet over medium-high heat. Stir-fry the chicken for about 5 minutes until cooked. Add the tomatoes, onion, and hot pepper, cooking for about 2 minutes more. Stir in hot prepared french fries and serve with a side of white rice. Garnish with cilantro.

ASIAN PINEAPPLE-MANGO FRIES

A flavorful sauce with a tropical twist.

1 recipe Essential Fries (page 16),
   Drive-in Fries (page 18), or
   Oven Fries (page 20)

1 fresh mango, diced

1 small can crushed
   pineapple, undrained

1 teaspoon honey

2 teaspoons fresh minced ginger

Combine all ingredients except fries in a food processor or blender and blend quickly so the mixture is not quite smooth. Serve on the side with prepared fries.

THAI SWEET CURRY FRIES

Green curry has a fresh, sweet taste that can't be replicated using a prepared sauce. This recipe evokes the flavors of green curry. For a variation, fresh basil can be substituted for the cilantro.

1 recipe Essential Fries (page 16), Oven Fries (page 20), or Homestyle Fries (page 25)

1 stalk lemon grass, minced

1 jalapeño, minced (less or more to taste)

3 cloves garlic, minced

2 teaspoons freshly grated ginger

1 cup chopped fresh cilantro

$1/2$ teaspoon ground cumin

1 teaspoon white pepper

$1/2$ teaspoon ground coriander

1 tablespoon soy sauce

2 tablespoons lime juice

2 teaspoons sugar

1 cup coconut milk

Place all ingredients except fries in a food processor or blender and process until smooth. Place the blended mixture in a saucepan and heat until just boiling. Serve over prepared french fries or use as a dipping sauce. Can be refrigerated up to one week.

VIETNAMESE FRENCH FRIES WITH BEEF

This recipe makes a fantastic main course that is quick to prepare when using frozen fries.

1 recipe Drive-in Fries (page 18)

1 yellow onion, thinly sliced

3 cloves garlic, minced

1 teaspoon vegetable oil

$1/2$ teaspoon sesame oil

1 (16-ounce) sirloin steak,
   cut into thin strips

$1/2$ cup matchstick carrots

2 teaspoons cornstarch

$1/2$ cup Nuoc Cham
   Sauce (page 100)

In a wok, sauté the onion and garlic over medium-high heat in the oils until they begin to soften, about 3 minutes. Add the steak strips and stir-fry for about 5 minutes until done. Add the carrots and briefly stir-fry.

Combine the cornstarch and Nuoc Cham Sauce. Pour over the steak and onions, and cook quickly to thicken, about 2 minutes. Add the french fries and stir to coat. Serve with additional Nuoc Cham Sauce to taste.

NUOC CHAM SAUCE

Nuoc Cham sauce is a versatile staple found in every Vietnamese kitchen.

$1/2$ cup sugar

1 cup water

2 tablespoons fish sauce

2 tablespoons rice vinegar

2 tablespoons lime juice

1 tablespoon red pepper flakes

2 cloves garlic, minced

Combine the sugar and water in a small saucepan and bring just to a boil. Remove from heat and add the remaining ingredients. Store in the refrigerator for up to two weeks. Makes about $1^1/2$ cups

ENGLISH FISH AND CHIPS

Thicker and more substantial than the American fry, the "chip," as it is known in Great Britain, is sold along with battered fish at "chippies" throughout England.

CHIPS

8 fresh Russet Burbank potatoes (8 to 10 ounces each)

Peanut oil

Sea salt

Peel and cut the potatoes into rough rectangular lengths, about $3/4$ x $1/2$ inch, using a knife with a sharp blade. Place the cut potatoes into a large bowl filled with cold water. Swirl the potatoes and drain the water. Spread the potatoes on a layer of paper towels and pat dry with additional paper towels.

In a large heavy pot or deep-fryer, preheat the peanut oil to 365 degrees F. Use a kitchen thermometer to verify the temperature. In small batches, approximately 2 cups each, add the sliced potatoes to the hot oil. Cook for 5 to 7 minutes until crisp. Using a basket, remove the potatoes from the oil, shaking to remove any excess. Spread the potatoes on a sheet pan lined with paper towels to drain. Sprinkle with sea salt.

Recipe continued on following page.

FISH

1 1/2 cups beer

2 cups flour

1 egg yolk, beaten

1/2 teaspoon white pepper

1/2 teaspoon salt

1/2 teaspoon black pepper

1/2 teaspoon baking powder

2 pounds cod fillets

Peanut oil

Malt vinegar

Whisk together all of the ingredients in a large bowl except the fish, peanut oil, and malt vinegar. In a deep-fryer, heat the peanut oil to 350 degrees F. Dredge the fish pieces in the batter and place in the oil using tongs. Cook about 5 minutes until golden and crisp. Fish may be held in a 225 degrees F oven while cooking the chips. Serve with malt vinegar. Serves 4

Dips and Sauces

FRY SAUCE

While ketchup is the de facto standard dipping accompaniment for the french fry, fry sauce is my personal choice. Served primarily in Idaho and Utah, where I grew up, fry sauce is a mixture of ketchup and mayo. I still remember as a teenager on a summer night at the local drive-in introducing the pink sauce to a girl from California I just met.

1 cup ketchup

1 cup mayonnaise

1 tablespoon sweet pickle relish

Mix all ingredients together until smooth and blended. Store in the refrigerator up to one week. Makes 2 cups

HOMEMADE KETCHUP

Ketchup doesn't have to come from a bottle with a three-year shelf life. This simple recipe is a base from which to experiment by varying and adding ingredients. Paired with Over Fries (page 20), you have a healthy delicious alternative to fast-food fries.

2 pounds fresh ripe tomatoes,
seeded and chopped

$1/2$ cup white vinegar

$1/4$ cup brown sugar

1 onion, chopped

1 clove garlic, minced

$1^1/2$ teaspoons salt

OPTIONAL INGREDIENTS

$1/4$ teaspoon ground allspice

2 tablespoons chopped
green chiles

2 tablespoons molasses

1 teaspoon cardamom

1 teaspoon cumin

1 teaspoon paprika

1 teaspoon red pepper flakes

Combine all but optional ingredients in a saucepan and cook over medium heat until onions are soft, about 15 minutes. Purée in a blender until smooth. Return mixture to the saucepan and continue to cook until thickened, about 15 minutes more. Let cool and store in the refrigerator up to two weeks.

Try adding one of the optional ingredients or any other flavors you wish. Makes about 3 to 4 cups

CARAMEL SAUCE

This is a quick and easy caramel sauce that is a great warm dipping treat to pair with Sweet Fries (page 22). As good as a dessert but with more vitamins.

1 cup sugar

1/4 cup water

1/4 cup butter

1/2 cup heavy cream

In a large heavy-bottomed saucepan, stir together the sugar and water. Cook over medium-high heat, without stirring, until it begins to boil. Do not stir or disturb the syrup until it becomes a dark amber color. Add the butter to the pan and whisk. Whisk in the heavy cream. The syrup will foam and expand. Remove from heat and continue to whisk until smooth. Pour into a glass container and let cool. Store in the refrigerator for up to two weeks.

Warm in the microwave for 30 seconds or as needed before serving with the Sweet Fries. Makes about 1 1/2 cups

BARBECUE MAYONNAISE

This is my wife Aimee's preferred dipping sauce for hot fries.

1 cup barbecue sauce

$1/2$ cup mayonnaise

Mix well. Store in the refrigerator up to one week. Makes $1^1/_2$ cups

BLUE CHEESE DIP

Cool buttermilk and tangy blue cheese is a classic combination. I prefer to a use a Gorgonzola cheese for its salty taste and slightly creamy texture.

1 cup mayonnaise

$1/2$ cup buttermilk

4 ounces blue cheese crumbles

$1/4$ teaspoon black pepper

Mix all ingredients together. May be stored for one week in the refrigerator. Makes about $1^1/_2$ cups

RANCH DRESSING

Fresh celery leaves provide a straight-from-the-garden taste to this fresh ranch dressing.

$3/4$ cup mayonnaise

$1/2$ cup buttermilk

2 tablespoons finely
    chopped fresh parsley

2 tablespoons finely
    chopped celery leaves

$1^1/2$ teaspoons fresh lemon juice

$3/4$ teaspoon onion powder

Combine all ingredients and chill in the refrigerator at least 1 hour. Keep refrigerated for up to two weeks. Makes about $1^1/4$ cups

TZATZIKI SAUCE

The famous Greek cucumber sauce that is good with gyros and great with fries

1 cup sour cream

1 cucumber, peeled, seeded, and chopped

1 tablespoon lemon juice

1 clove garlic, diced

$1/2$ teaspoon salt

$1/2$ teaspoon pepper

1 teaspoon fresh dill

Place all ingredients in a food processor and blend until combined. Refrigerate before serving for the best flavor. Can be stored up to one week. Makes about $1^1/2$ cups

SATAY SAUCE

Creamy and rich in peanut flavor, this is a great satay sauce for dipping fries or for mixing with cooked flat noodles for a quick Thai lunch.

1 (10-ounce) can coconut milk

1/2 cup peanut butter

1 tablespoon tamari soy sauce

2 teaspoons brown sugar

1/2 teaspoon red chili paste

In a saucepan combine the ingredients and bring just to a boil, stirring frequently. Remove from heat and keep warm until serving. May be refrigerated up to one week and warmed to serve. Makes 2 cups

SPECIAAL SAUCE

This creation is a staple of the ubiquitous *frietkot*, or fry stand, in Belgium and Holland. Simple, yet very tasty.

1/4 cup finely chopped onion

1/4 cup pickle relish

1/2 cup ketchup

1/2 cup mayonnaise

Mix all ingredients together and serve. May be refrigerated up to one week. Makes about 1 1/4 cups

CURRY KETCHUP

Probably my favorite ketchup recipe, this is easy to make and unexpectedly different.

$1/2$ teaspoon curry powder

$1/4$ teaspoon ground turmeric

1 clove garlic, crushed

$1/2$ cup ketchup (may use
   Homemade Ketchup page 107)

$1/2$ cup mayonnaise

Mix all ingredients and let sit 30 minutes before serving. May be refrigerated up to one week. Makes about 1 cup

HORSERADISH SAUCE

Mayo with a bite of horseradish—perfect with simple flavors such as Fresh Green Bean Fries (page 44).

1 teaspoon prepared horseradish

1 cup mayonnaise

2 teaspoons chopped
   fresh cilantro

Combine all ingredients and mix well. Makes about $1^{1}/_{4}$ cups

WASABI GARLIC MAYONNAISE

Serve with fries or Tempura Vegetables (page 82) as an Asian-inspired dipping sauce.

2 tablespoons toasted sesame oil

2 teaspoons minced garlic

2 teaspoons minced ginger

$^1/_4$ cup mayonnaise

$^1/_2$ cup sour cream

2 teaspoons prepared
   wasabi powder

2 teaspoons tamari soy sauce

Heat the sesame oil in a small skillet over medium-low heat. Add the ginger and garlic, sautéing until crispy and translucent. Do not burn the garlic. Set aside.

In a food processor, combine the mayonnaise, sour cream, wasabi powder, soy sauce, and sautéed ginger and garlic mixture. Mix until smooth. Makes about 1 cup

TERIYAKI MAYONNAISE

Perfect for dipping Sweet Fries (page 22) or Tofu Fries (page 68).

1 cup mayonnaise

1/2 cup prepared teriyaki sauce

1 teaspoon toasted sesame seeds

Combine the teriyaki sauce and the mayonnaise in a bowl. Garnish with toasted sesame seeds before serving. Makes 1 1/2 cups

SWEET ONION MAYONNAISE

This mayo is best enjoyed after an overnight stay in the refrigerator to allow the flavors to blend.

1/4 cup finely chopped sweet onion

1/4 cup mayonnaise

1/2 cup sour cream

1 tablespoon white vinegar

2 teaspoons celery salt

1 teaspoon dry mustard

Mix all ingredients together and refrigerate at least 1 hour before serving. Store in the refrigerator for up to one week. Makes about 1 cup

ROASTED GARLIC MAYO

Roasting whole heads of garlic is an easy way to unlock a more nuanced flavor that comes as the sugars are caramelized.

2 heads garlic

1 teaspoon olive oil

1 cup mayonnaise

$1/2$ teaspoon ground black pepper

Preheat the oven to 400 degrees F. Cut off the tops of the whole garlic, leaving the cloves exposed, but do not remove any skin. Drizzle $1/2$ teaspoon olive oil on each whole garlic. Wrap the garlic in aluminum foil and bake for 40 minutes. Remove and allow to cool.

Unwrap garlic from the foil. Remove the roasted cloves from the skin and mash. Mix with the mayonnaise and black pepper. Serve immediately or refrigerate up to one week. Makes about $1^1/2$ cups

RASPBERRY GINGER DIPPING SAUCE

Sweet and flavorful especially when eaten with hot and crisp Tofu Fries (page 68).

1 cup seedless raspberry jam

1 teaspoon soy sauce

1 teaspoon brown sugar

1 teaspoon fresh minced ginger

Add all ingredients to a saucepan. Bring to a boil, stirring until thickened. Cool and serve as a dipping sauce. Maybe be refrigerated up to one week. Makes about 1 cup

LEMON BUTTER SAUCE

An elegant dipping sauce for Oven Asparagus Fries (page 59) that also works well as an accompaniment to broiled salmon.

2 tablespoons melted butter

2 tablespoons lemon juice

$1/2$ cup mayonnaise

2 teaspoons Dijon mustard

Mix all ingredients and serve immediately. Makes about 1 cup

Index

Metric Conversion Chart

Volume Measurements

U.S.	Metric
1 teaspoon	5 ml
1 tablespoon	15 ml
1/4 cup	60 ml
1/3 cup	75 ml
1/2 cup	125 ml
2/3 cup	150 ml
3/4 cup	175 ml
1 cup	250 ml

Weight Measurements

U.S.	Metric
1/2 ounce	15 g
1 ounce	30 g
3 ounces	90 g
4 ounces	115 g
8 ounces	225 g
12 ounces	350 g
1 pound	450 g
2 1/4 pounds	1 kg

Temperature Conversion

Fahrenheit	Celsius
250	120
300	150
325	160
350	180
375	190
400	200
425	220
450	230